Travel Size Doodle Colouring Book

Flowers

Collection of 5 hand drawn flower doodles

Kristiina Jefimova

The idea for this book came to me when I was on holiday in Alicante, Spain. I thought it would be good to create travel size versions of my doodles. Also, since there is so much to do and explore in our holiday destinations, I decided to limit the amount of doodles to 5 per book. Best results can be achieved by using colouring pencils. I dedicate this colouring book series to my parents. Thank you for spending a lovely holiday with me.

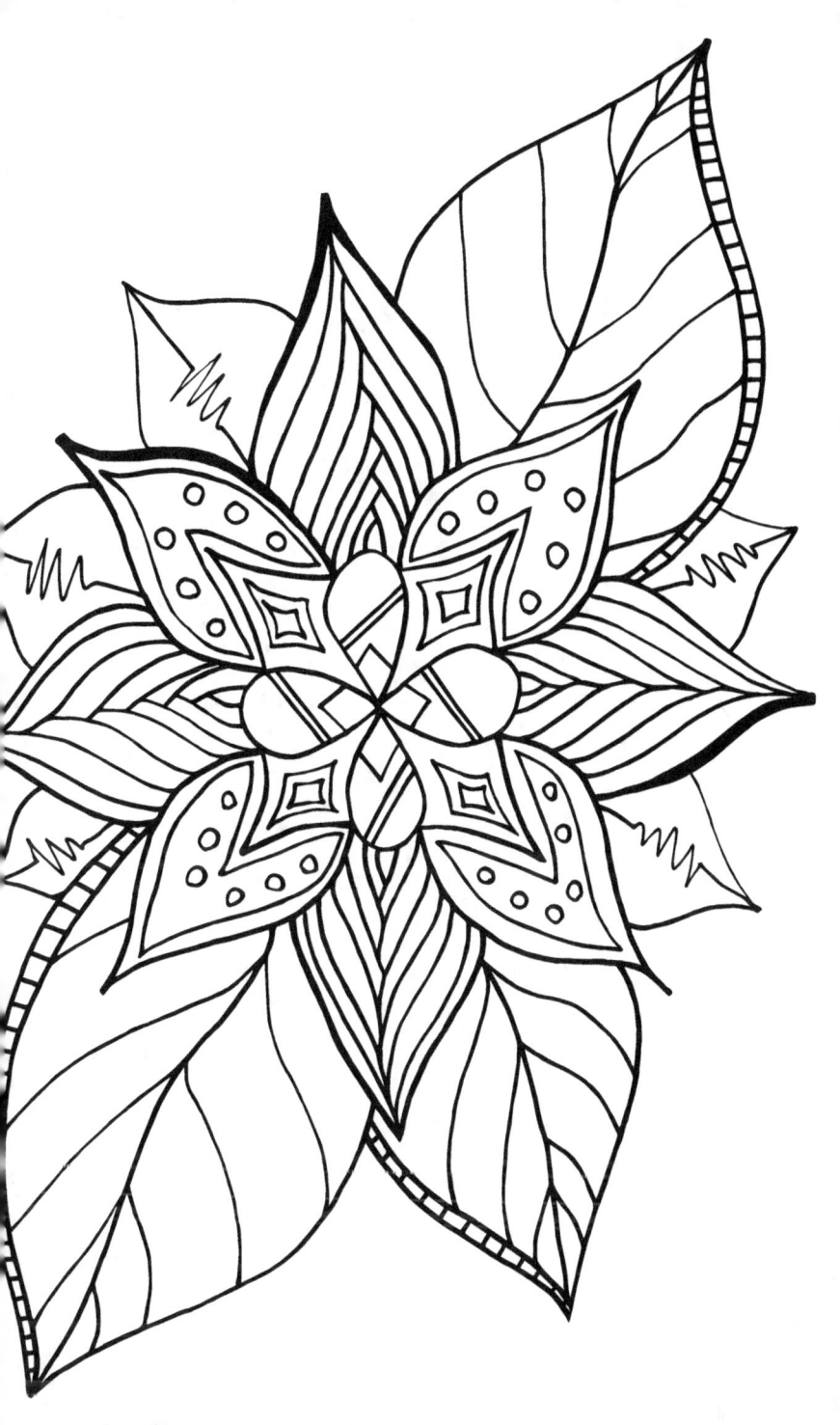

Flowers

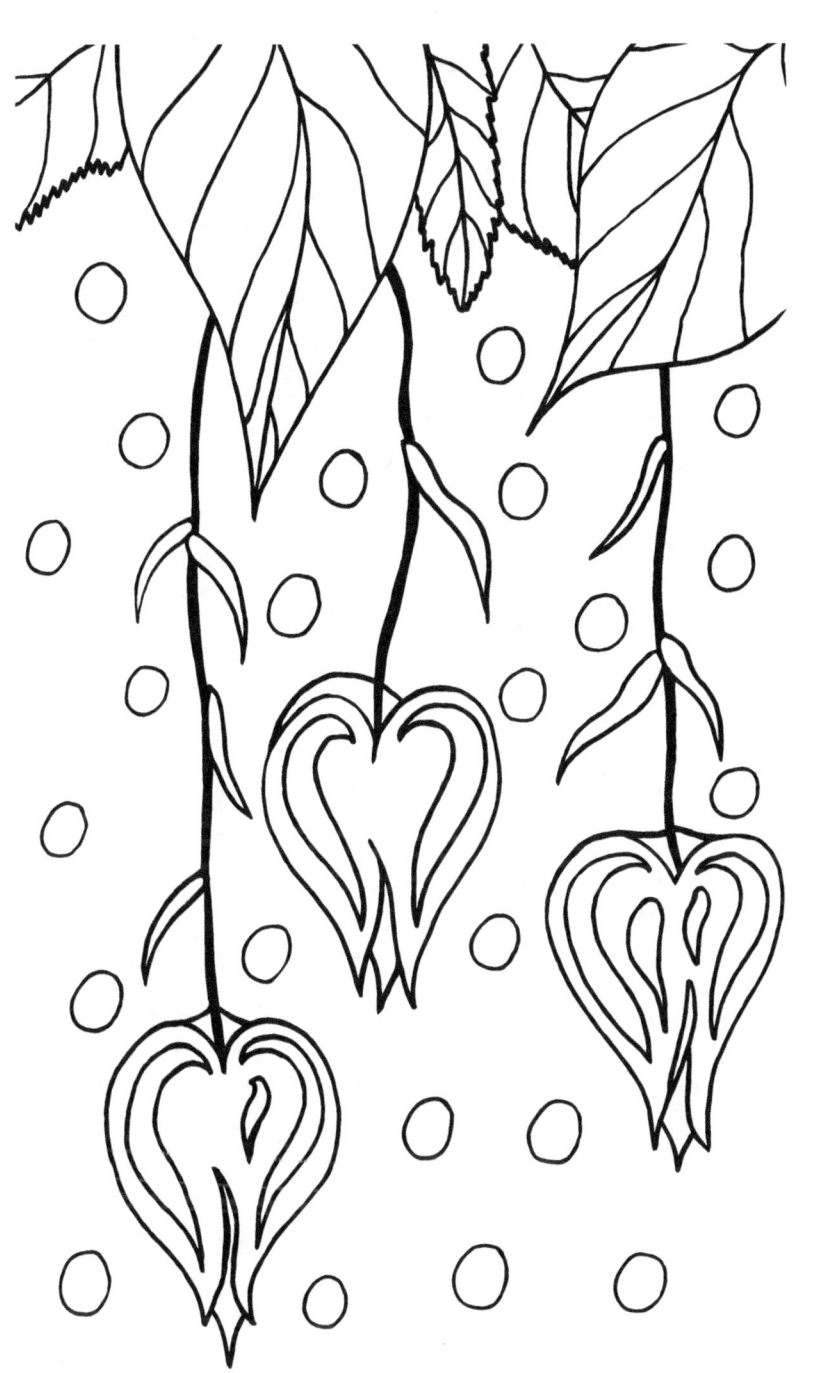

Flowers

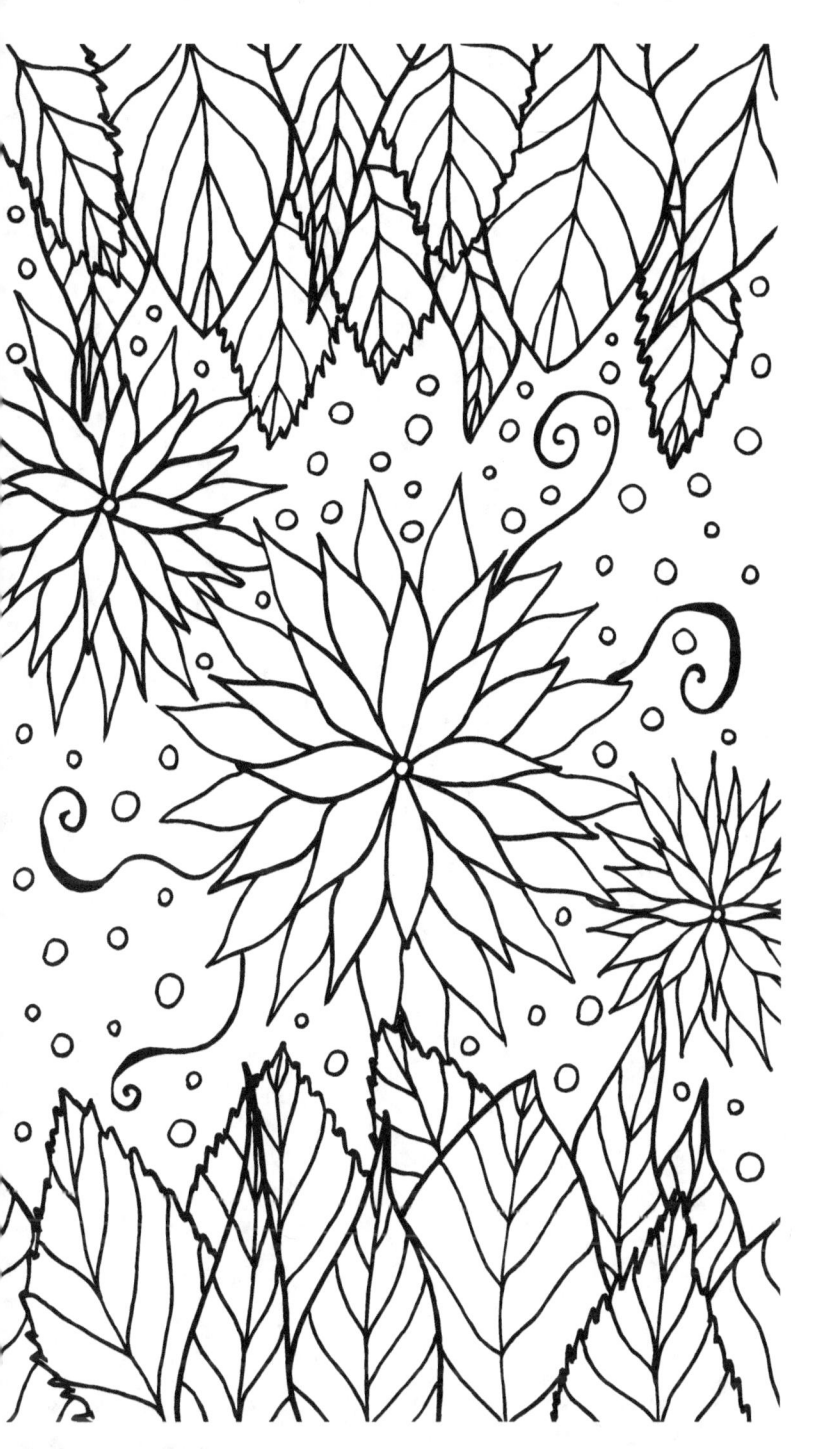

Flowers

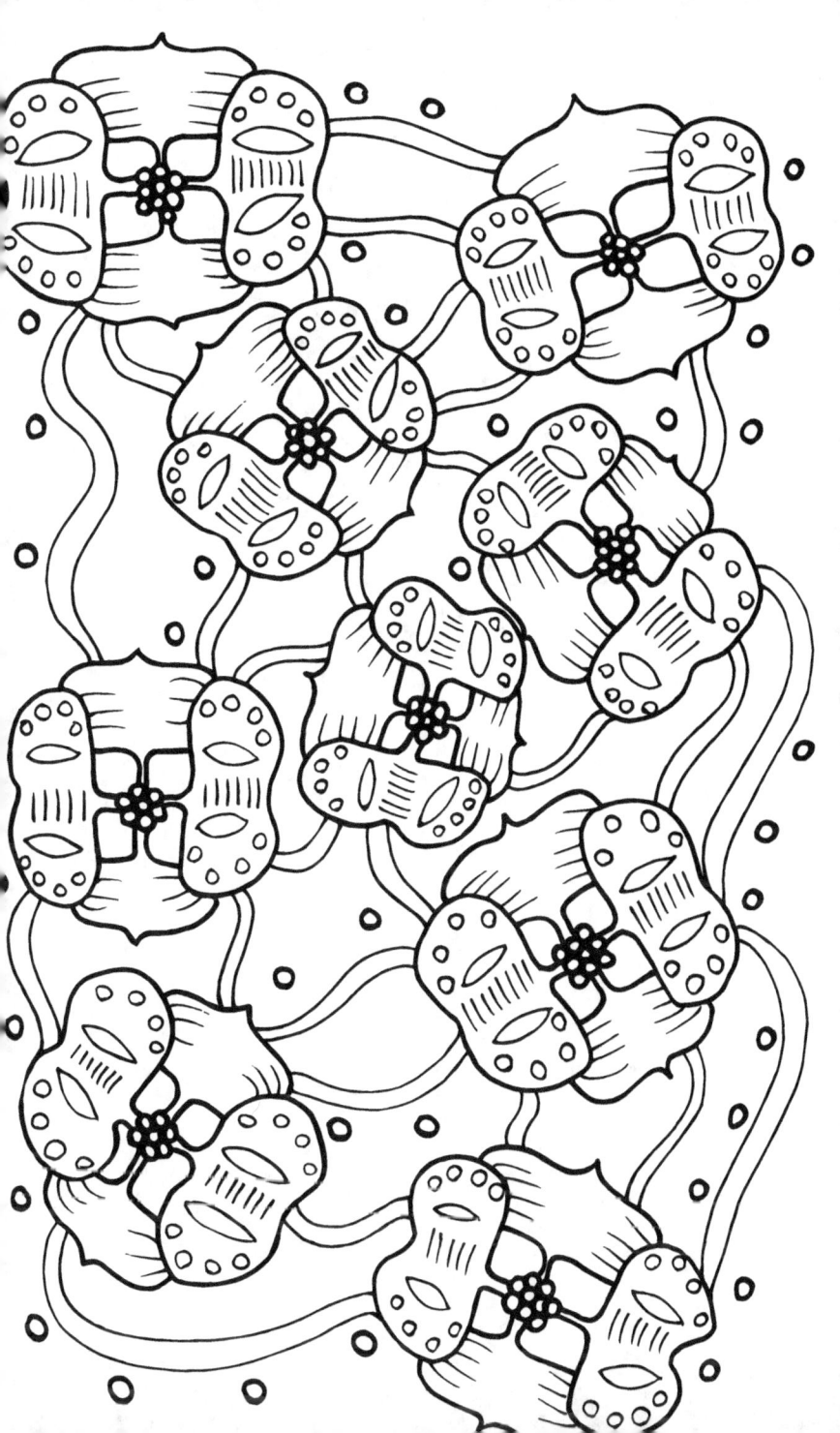

Flowers

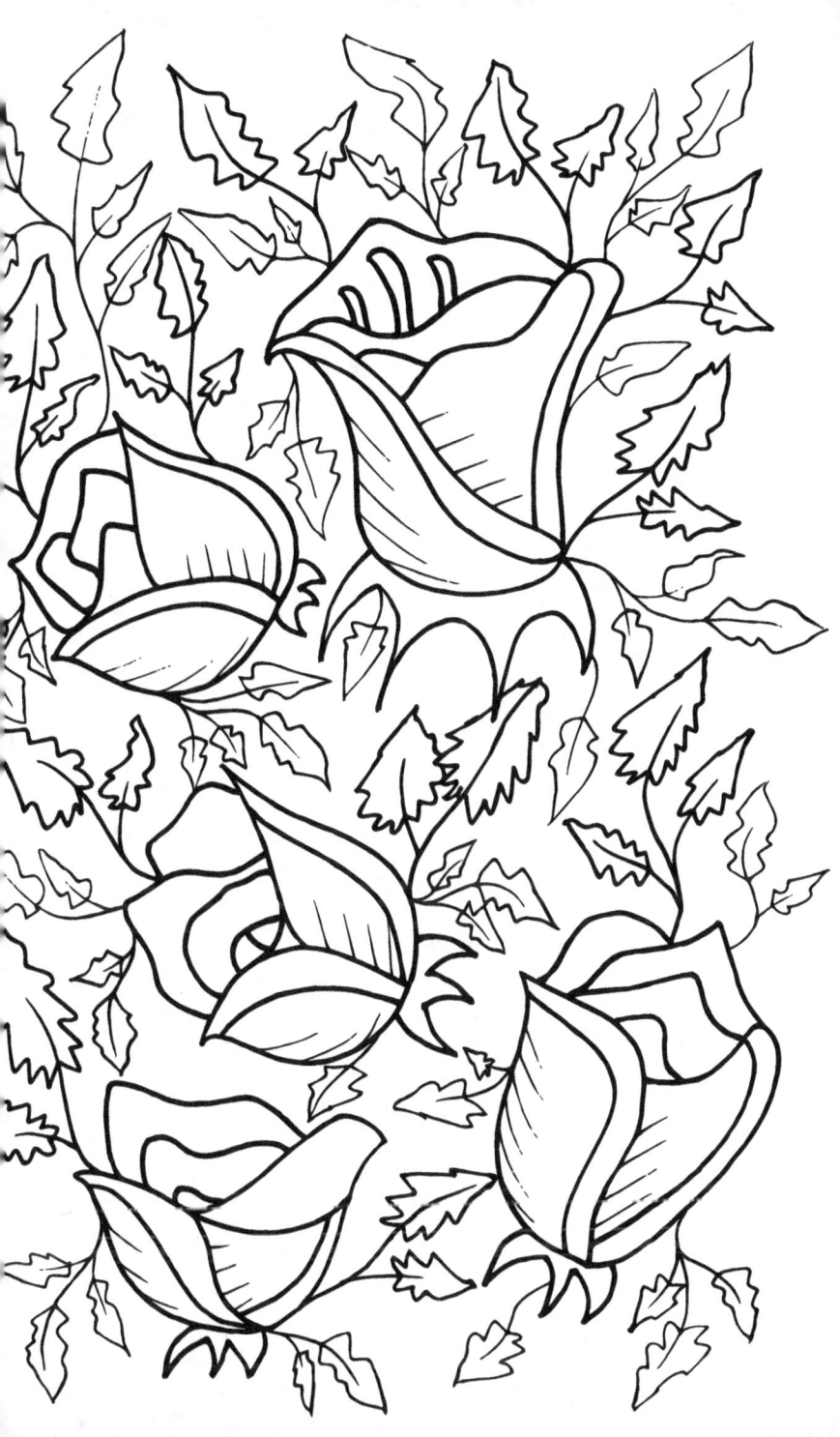

If you enjoyed this colouring book and would like to explore more of my artwork please don't hesitate to check out my Instagram (jkcreativeflow) and YouTube channel (Kristiina J). All doodles from this book and previous books are available as prints on various products on Redbubble (JKCreativeFlow). More colouring books available on Amazon, including the first Travel Size Doodle Colouring Book: Leaves, the second Travel Size Doodle Colouring Book: Eyes and the third Travel Size Doodle Colouring Book: Abstract.

Next themes in the Travel Size Doodle Colouring Book series:
- Mandalas
- Ladders

www.ingramcontent.com/pod-product-compliance
Lightning Source LLC
Chambersburg PA
CBHW071205220526
45468CB00003B/1171